# PUERTO RICO:
# Fools Gold or
# Gold Mine?

I0487193

AUTHORS:
Tanya Rodriguez
Luis A. del Mazo, Jr.

# Disclaimer

# PuErTo RiCo: FOOls GOld or Gold MINe?

# Table of Contents

# Chapter 1: Puerto Rico

Puerto Rico is a territory of the United States, that, together with a 143 few smaller sister islands including Mona, Culebra, and Vieques, is known for its diverse and beautiful landscape. This landscape varies from the white sand beaches like those at Mosquito Bay in Vieques to the only Tropical rainforest in the U.S. like the famous El Yunque. The culture of Puerto Rico is diverse, blending Latin, Caribbean, and American traditions. English and Spanish are the two main languages in Puerto Rico.

The territory is connected to the mainland and has a strong and robust tourism industry. It boasts 25 golf courses and hosts the Puerto Rico Open. Puerto Rico is currently looking to add 30,000 additional vacation units to compete with the neighboring island of Dominican Republic.

In 2017, Puerto Rico was devastated by Hurricane Maria. Since then it has recovered, and the government has offered tax incentives to aid in the recovery of the territory. Currently, many real estate investors are considering investing in Puerto Rico. If you are one of them, you need to know whether you should put your money in Puerto Rican real estate or not. Let us help you out, by laying out all the facts.

This book is going to help guide you into deciding whether investing in Puerto Rico is worth or not. Let us help you analyze the benefits, risks and rewards of investing in the Island and share some tips for making a good sound investment.

# Chapter 2: Real Estate Investment in Puerto Rico

Since the destruction of Hurricane Maria, Investors have been concerned about the lasting effects of the devastation on its real estate sector. Although the hurricane caused destruction, the real estate industry of Puerto Rico can still prove to be lucrative. Researchers who evaluated the effects of Hurricane Maria on Puerto Rican real estate uncovered that the hurricane contributed to the downward trend of housing prices by 15% on the territory. Properties in Puerto Rico are now worth half what they were nine years ago. Moreover, the interest of Investors in Puerto Rico's Real estate is rising, as indicated by online searches for Real Estate. Based on a survey carried out by Point2homes, many home buyers are looking to buy low-priced homes on the island.

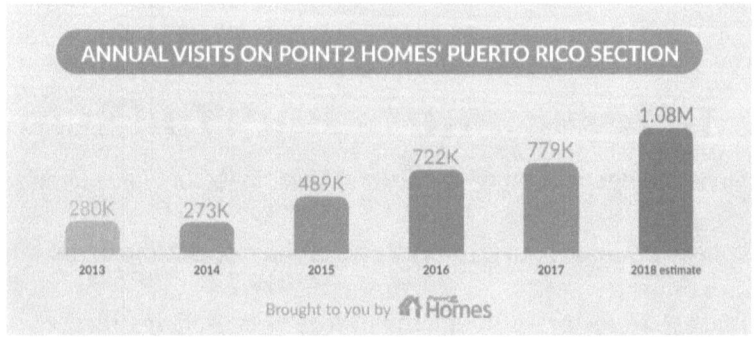

## Destruction by Hurricane Maria

Hurricane Maria caused damage of around $90 billion. About $37 billion worth of damage was recorded in the housing sector. More than 470,000 properties were caught in the storm and out of these, a fifth were destroyed entirely while the rest were severely damaged. The New York Times reported that over 16,000 residents were facing foreclosure before the storm, and only 65 percent of all houses in Puerto Rico are registered.

The economic recession has already been troubling Puerto Rico for the past ten years. The median home prices were already beginning to drop, and Hurricane Maria only helped contribute to this current downward trend.

Within the past eight years, the median home sales prices in Puerto Rico have decreased by 48 percent. Amongst all the markets analyzed by point2homes, the most significant price depreciation was in Aguadilla and Humacao. Humacao is ground zero for the hurricane, and it experienced the highest drop in value between the years 2016 and 2018.

Guaynabo and Rincon did not experience the same depreciation as the rest of the island, and as a result, the homes in these areas are currently the most expensive. Ponce, Fajardo, and Arecibo offer affordable options with homes at half the cost than what they were eight years ago.

San Juan is another popular destination, and it experienced a 59 percent drop in real estate since the recession began in 2008. The median home price here has decreased from $265,000 to $107,450.

# PUERTO RICO HOUSING MARKET

| Market | 2018 Median Home Price | 2016 Median Home Price | 2013 Median Home Price | 2010 Median Home Price | 2010/2018 Price Change |
|---|---|---|---|---|---|
| Puerto Rico overall | $116,750 | $144,900 | $175,000 | $224,000 | -48% |
| Humacao | $97,250 | $250,000 | $280,000 | $369,000 | -74% |
| Aguadilla | $99,000 | $185,000 | $200,000 | $375,000 | -74% |
| Rio Grande | $124,500 | $226,500 | $260,000 | $325,000 | -62% |
| Carolina | $91,000 | $139,500 | $180,000 | $235,000 | -61% |
| Dorado | $190,000 | $415,000 | $359,500 | $475,000 | -60% |
| San Juan | $107,450 | $200,000 | $250,000 | $265,000 | 59% |
| Fajardo | $79,500 | $129,000 | $139,000 | $167,000 | -52% |
| Ponce | $86,000 | $97,450 | $149,500 | $160,000 | -46% |
| Arecibo | $78,500 | $100,000 | $124,900 | $145,000 | -46% |
| Bayamon | $99,000 | $113,600 | $130,000 | $169,000 | -41% |
| Mayaguez | $126,950 | $130,000 | $175,000 | $210,000 | -40% |
| Caguas | $128,000 | $135,450 | $156,500 | $198,000 | -35% |
| Cabo Rojo | $175,000 | $175,000 | $200,000 | $230,000 | -24% |
| Isabela | $174,900 | $180,000 | $195,000 | $227,000 | -23% |
| Guaynabo | $248,000 | $262,250 | $270,000 | $290,000 | -14% |
| Rincon | $230,000 | $240,000 | $252,500 | $265,000 | -13% |

Brought to you by **Homes**

## Interest in Puerto Rico's Real Estate Grew After Hurricane Maria

About 95 percent of all people who are shopping for homes start their search online. So, for determining the interest of people in purchasing homes in Puerto Rico, researchers turned to Google. Google Trends showed that the interest in the island's real estate market had grown after Hurricane Maria. Traffic figures from Point2 Homes have also showed that more people were searching for homes to buy after the storm.

Researchers also surveyed all the users who were visiting Point2 Homes' Puerto Rico section. Based on the results of the survey, researchers determined that Puerto Rico is still an attractive real estate market for American buyers looking to buy low-priced homes. Out of all the survey respondents, 60 percent were interested in buying a home in Puerto Rico, while 34 percent just wanted to see the prices. The reasons of the respondents for looking up houses in Puerto Rico were diverse — some were looking for investment opportunities, few were after vacation homes while some already had family and friends living there. 78 percent of participants said that the homes in Puerto Rico were on their radar even before the storm hit.

## Real Estate Agents' Perspective

Puerto Rico's real estate professionals, are optimistic about the rehabilitation of the Real Estate market. They believe that even though the hurricane was an unfortunate event, it still brought some real estate opportunities with it. Those opportunities are low-priced homes and an active rental market that are attracting more global investors.

The consensus is that many homes are way undervalued, especially Multi-family and commercial investments. In many cases, the replacement cost of the structure is way more than the actual purchase price. Depreciated values make it an excellent opportunity to invest in the vacation rental market.

Puerto Rico is in one of the few opportunity zones to offer these types of vacation rental opportunities at extreme discounts.

# Chapter 3: Benefits of Investing in Puerto Rico Real Estate

Hurricane Maria caused massive destruction in Puerto Rico. Even before the storm, the island was combating the financial crisis. On the surface, everything looked bad for the island. However, as we saw in the last chapter, things aren't as bad as they may seem, and Puerto Rico has turned into a right place for real estate investment. Puerto Rico is as a new phoenix rising by Rich Holman, the founder of Institution and Residential Sales at Far International. He said that if one studies hurricanes, the past has revealed that islands and countries hit by a hurricane rebuilt better than ever.

It turns out that Holman was right. Flimsy buildings were destroyed by the hurricane, which left room for stronger homes with more comprehensive building codes. After the hurricane, Puerto Rico has the opportunity to rebuild the whole infrastructure strategically from scratch. Now, about two years after the hurricane hit, Puerto Rico is an excellent place for real estate investment. Let's look at some benefits of investing in Puerto Rico real estate.

- **Tax Incentives**

In 2012, several tax loopholes were introduced by Puerto Rico to lure businesses and real-estate investors. Due to these tax incentives, businesses and investors can make healthy profits from working and investing in Puerto Rico. See the key incentives below:

**Act 20 or the Export Services Act**

Act 20 provides tax incentives to specific firms that move their business to Puerto Rico. Under this act, companies that qualify are taxed 4 percent. Moreover, they are exempt from property taxes and get to enjoy tax exemption on capital gains, interest, and dividends.

**Act 22 or the Individual Investors Act**

This act awards people who gain residency in Puerto Rico a zero-percent personal tax rate. Under the Individual Investors Act, individuals enjoy 100-percent tax exemption on certain capital gains, interest, and dividends. To qualify for the tax benefits offered by the Act 22, investors must be residents of Puerto Rico or must become one.

- **Opportunity Zone**

There are currently 8,700 opportunity zones in the U.S. opportunity zones are economically-distressed communities nominated by the State Governor for designation and certified by the Secretary of the U.S. Treasury are called Opportunity Zones. The goal behind creating Opportunity Zones is to attract people towards infrastructure, small business, and housing investments in areas that are economically depressed.

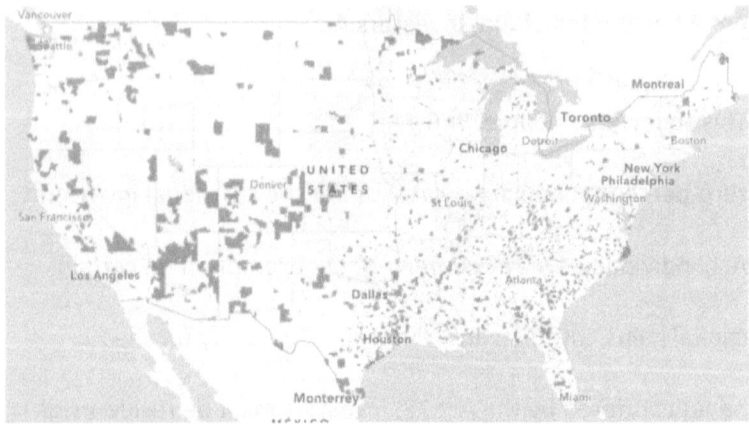

Financial Accounts of the United States data to calculate that

U.S. households were sitting on $2.3 trillion in unrealized capital

gains in stocks and funds alone at the end of 2015. Fast-forward

to the end of 2017 — a stock market boom later — and that

figure climbed to $3.8 trillion. If you include U.S. corporations,

which analysts conservatively estimate held $2.3 trillion in

unrealized capital gains on their books at the end of 2017, the

pot of potential capital eligible for reinvestment in Opportunity

Zones climbs to a total of $6.1 trillion.

U.S. investors have the choice to defer capital gains for 5, 7 or 10 years if they reinvest and hold the profits in the Opportunity Zone. Opportunities Zones decreases the taxes on such capital gains by 10 percent and 15 percent if held by the investor for five or seven years, respectively. Moreover, investors are provided a full exemption from capital gains tax on all their future capital gains from investments if they hold those investments for ten years. Anyone level of investor can invest in opportunity zones not just accredited investors.

Some significant benefits that investors get from putting their money into an Opportunity Zone include:

- Gains from selling any capital asset such as stocks, bonds and real estate, can be rolled into Opportunity Zone investment.
- Investors can benefit from the Opportunity Zone's remarkable tax benefits by only reinvesting the gains rather than the entire proceeds they get from selling an asset.

- Opportunity Zone benefits are available to more wide-ranging businesses compared to several other incentives programs introduced in the past and include investments like rental property businesses.

One of the best ways of taking advantage of Opportunity Zones is to purchase older buildings there, renovate them, and then rent them out.

Almost the entire island of Puerto Rico is now an Opportunity Zone, which means that you can gain favorable tax benefits if you invest in the real estate properties in Puerto Rico. Consumers can be confident that the same property rights that govern the mainland are the same rights that govern in Puerto Rico. You can minimize capital gains tax by keeping your reinvested capital within Puerto Rico.

Since Puerto Rico is a U.S. territory, it enjoys economic and legal benefits that aren't available to other neighboring Caribbean islands.

You might think that other Opportunity Zones provide the same benefits, so why should you invest in Puerto Rico real estate? Well, a history of economic crisis, coupled with Hurricane Maria, has resulted in favorable market conditions for real estate investors. You can acquire real estate properties on the island at a bargain price right now. The Real Estate prices in Puerto Rico are much lower than similar properties in other areas. Moreover, Puerto Rico also has a robust tourist industry since it is easily accessible by U.S. citizens.

## Act-185 – Private Equity Funds Act

There was a time when hedge funds and private equity funds were practically non-existent in Puerto Rico. However, this changed on 12th November 2014 when Puerto Rico's governor signed act 185 or the Private Equity Funds Act. This act grants special tax treatment to the funds that meet its requirements and to their general partners and investors.

The two types of funds that qualify for special tax treatment under the Act 185 include Puerto Rico Private Equity Funds (PRPEF) and Private Equity Funds (PEF). Each must:

- Have an office within the territory of Puerto Rico
- Invest at least 80% of its paid-in capital (cash equivalents and cash excluded) in securities that are issued by entities which at the time of acquisition not listed on stock exchange markets in the U.S. or any other foreign country
- Invest the paid-in excess capital in specific short-term securities as well as obligations of the United States government or the government of Puerto Rico, short term repurchase agreements with specific institutions, FDIC-insured CDs, deposit and checking accounts and some other specific investments
- To participate in this tax exemption, investors must qualify as accredited investors.

- Use investment advisor that has a business office located in Puerto Rico, is engaged in business or trade inside Puerto Rico and is registered with relevant authorities to operate as diversified investment funds. In other words, before four years from the date of organization, less than 20 percent of the capital of a qualifying fund may be invested in one business

- Have at least $10 million capital before 24 months after the issuance of its membership or partnership interests and each following year.

- Moreover, at least one of its limited partners or investors must be assigned to an advisory board.

Investors in the Puerto Rico Private Equity Funds are eligible for more beneficial tax treatments than those in the Private Equity Funds. Investors of the qualifying fund are partners in a partnership. The Fund won't be subject to income tax on its capital gains or dividend income and interest. Investors are responsible for a distributive share of income that comes from a qualifying fund. Income that investors derive from dividends and interest is subject to a 10 percent income tax. Capital gains that an investor gets from the qualifying fund are subject to 10 percent income tax. However, if the capital is coming from sources in Puerto Rico, it is exempt from income tax.

Capital gains that an investor realizes upon selling the shares of the qualifying fund are subject to a 5 percent income tax unless they reinvest the capital in a Puerto Rico Private Equity Fund within 90 days. In this case, capital gains won't be subject to any income tax.

Property owned by qualifying funds is exempt from the property taxes. Investors who live in Puerto Rico and invest in Private Equity Fund can deduct up to 30 percent of their initial investment within ten years provided that their maximum deduction doesn't exceed 15 percent of their income before deduction.

Investors who live in Puerto Rico and invest in Puerto Rico Private Equity Fund can deduct up to 60 percent of their initial investment within 15 years provided that their maximum deduction doesn't exceed 30 percent of their net income before deduction.

**Bonus Tax incentive acts:**

**Act 74** works in cooperation with the other tax vehicles to enhance a funds potential for maximum high yield growth. The Government of the Commonwealth of Puerto Rico, through the Puerto Rico Tourism Company, provides incentives for the development of world-class tourism activities. The benefits under this law will remain valid for a period of 10 years from the starting date of the eligible tourism-related project, and the business operation will be entitled to a 10-year extension.

Incentives

- A tax credit equal to 10% of the total project costs, or 50% of the cash investment made by investors (whichever is less)

- A tax credit equal to 40% of the eligible investment, the first tranche at the second year of operation, and the rest in subsequent years.

- Tax credit equal to 30% of the eligible investment, first 10% percent at the moment to obtain the finance, the other 20% percent the first tranche the year that receive the first paying guest and the rest in subsequent years.

- 100% exemption on municipal construction excise taxes, Vieques and Culebra 75%

- 100% exemption on sales and uses taxes

- 100% exemption on excise taxes and other municipal taxes for new projects or 90% exemption, if the existing project, Vieques and Culebra 75%

- 90% exemption on income tax or 100% exemption if the project is located in the island municipalities of Vieques or Culebra

- Up to 90% exemption on personal an real property municipal taxes, Vieques and Culebra 75%

## Eligible Businesses

- Hotels, condo-hotels, small inns ("Paradores"), guest houses, timeshares and vacation clubs, including the operation of casinos.

- Theme parks, golf courses operated by or associated with a hotel that is an exempt business, tourism marinas and docking facilities for tourists.

- Natural resources that are useful as a source of active or passive entertainment or amusement.

- Other facilities or activities that, due to the special attractive features deriving from their usefulness as a source of active or passive entertainment or amusement constitute a stimulus to domestic or foreign tourists.

| Act 185 Funds | Both funds | Opportunity Funds |
|---|---|---|
| Only for Accredited investors | Only Accredited investors can invest in opportunity funds | Anyone can invest in opportunity zone and not exclusive to accredited investors |
| 1-year minimum holding period unless fund qualifies for the 90-day rule. | Beneficiaries subject to taxes of the jurisdiction of residence. | The 5, 7 and 10 yr. holding are for tax benefits |
| Funds can be deployed anywhere on Island of Puerto Rico. | Can couple Act No. 74 the Tourism Development Act for Bonus incentives. | Can only be deployed in designated zones within US jurisdiction. |

# Chapter 4: Risks of Investing in Puerto Rico

Since Puerto Rico is still recovering from the hurricane, there are certain risks involved with real estate investments in Puerto Rico. Some significant risks you should be aware of before deciding to invest in Puerto Rico include:

- **Many Locals have Left Puerto Rico**

The storm devastated Puerto Rico and a majority of the locals left due to lack of aid, slow recovery, and massive unemployment. In other words, this means that it could be hard for you to find people who would want to rent your residential or commercial investment property.

- **Power Grid Issue**

Hurricane destroyed the power grid and it took more than 9 months to make it operational again. The fragile system was exposed again when a power outage hit Puerto Rico last year. So there is a high risk of power grid failure in the future.

However, most power failures in the central districts are temporary.

- ## Debt Crisis

Another significant risk to consider is that Puerto Rico is in a severe debt crisis. The main reason real estate prices on the island have plummeted by as much as 25 percent in the last few years. Due to the low real estate prices, you could snag a good deal. However, since the economic climate of Puerto Rico is unstable, it could be a risky investment. However, If the government can take steps to solve the crisis, and the situation of Puerto Rico stabilizes, then these investments can work in your favor, and you may profit substantially from your investment.

Consider the risks before investing in Puerto Rico's real estate market. If you decide to invest, then consider going the vacation rental industry route. Despite what the economic condition of the state is in, tourist dollars are always welcome and residential vacation rentals are rapidly dominating global

tourism markets.

# Chapter 5: Tips for Buying Property in Puerto Rico

If you want to purchase a real estate property on Puerto Rico for investment, follow these essential tips:

- ## Work with Real Estate Agents

There aren't many buyer's agents active in Puerto Rico as brokers acquire listings on their own and steer potential buyers their way. When you are searching for a property to buy in Puerto Rico, several agents need to be involved. A broker can show you all of their exclusive listings, but not all the listing on the market, so multiple agents will be necessary.

As with any property purchase, it is good to work with reputable agents or nationally recognized firms. Local databases that you should check out include the Multiple Listing Service of Puerto Rico. Other comprehensives websites that can assist you include Clasificadosonline.com and Point2Homes.com. These databases might not be up to date.

Therefore you should use agents who work in the area where you are looking to buy an investment property. They can advise on cultural issues, local lifestyle, and pricing. You can find reputable agents in Puerto Rico by asking around the local communities. If you want to do a property search without a real estate agent's assistance, you must know Spanish. That's because not everyone in Puerto Rico speaks English fluently.

- **Research**

If you are thinking to invest in the real estate market of Puerto Rico, you must do thorough research, especially if you aren't familiar with the local market. Third-party services like Point2Homes and TasaMax provide comprehensive sales data that you can use to research the market of Puerto Rico. If you are interested in any property, you should obtain a complete report on it.

- **Consider the Costs of Property Management**

Before purchasing a property, determine how you are going to manage it and the costs associated with the management. For instance, the homeowners association fee (HOA) typically covers a building's general maintenance and any shared facilities and areas.

- **Consider the Financing Options**

There isn't any obligation to purchase real estate property in Puerto Rico in cash. You can obtain a home equity loan on your existing property for rental property investment in Puerto Rico. Local lending is another option. Just make sure to be prepared for a large amount of paperwork.

- **Take Advantage of Tax Breaks**

We have already discussed the tax incentives you get for investing in Puerto Rico. Make sure to make the most of these incentives when you are buying real estate property for investment. Work with an experienced financial advisor who can guide you on tax-related matters and help you make the most of the tax incentives available in the opportunity zone.

# Chapter 6: Is Puerto Rico Worth It?

One of the best things about getting involved in the real estate property business in an area like Puerto Rico is that it provides you an opportunity of exploring a location that you might never have thought about seeing previously. Also, it gives you the chance to start small – since the property prices are low – and work your way up from there. When you want to invest in Puerto Rico, the first most crucial thing to consider is the costs of property in the area. We have discussed the property prices in Puerto Rico and showed you how much they have depreciated compared to other regions of the United States. Many areas on the island still haven't recovered from the damage. Thus the reason there is a large inventory of real estate available for sale, and much of it is significantly inexpensive. It seems like Puerto Rico is a gold mine right now, and the low property prices are enough to get people excited, but what does it mean for you? Be prepared that you are likely going to have to do a lot of work on the property you buy in Puerto Rico.

Right now, you can buy a property in Puerto Rico for one-third of what you would have had to pay before Hurricane Maria. It's a great time to buy a real estate in Puerto Rico, but only if you can make significant repairs to the property. In some cases, a teardown of the whole structure is required, and the permit process can be complicated and lengthy. Moreover, some of the buildings there haven't been repaired yet. While some areas of the island have improved, other areas are still devastated.

You could also consider things like offices, schools and other amenities if you are serious about buying property in Puerto Rico. However, again, you should remember that the storm has severely impacted all these things. It is almost impossible to determine how the affected areas will grow in the future. A good rule of thumb we recommend you to use is that if a particular section of Puerto Rico was affluent before the storm, then it's a good chance it will reacquire its status in the future.

However, if the section you are targeting was impoverished before the storm, then it probably won't become affluent in the future after the area has recovered from the damage.

Puerto Rico is, without a doubt a beautiful location that is well worth investing, provided you know what you are doing. Investing in Puerto Rico is not ideal for the novice investor. However, if you are well-versed in the real estate business, then you can get some great deals in Puerto Rico. The most important thing is that you do your research and determine what you are getting into before you put your money on the line. At the moment, investing in real estate in Puerto Rico could be one of the soundest financial investments in your life, or it could be your biggest mistake. That might look like a vague description of Puerto Rico, but it is the truth. In the end, everything boils down to the location and allocation of the property you are buying. Buying properties in Puerto Rico with the right investment strategies could be worth it as long as you have a plan and exit strategy in place.

# Chapter 7: Conclusion

There are currently an estimated 6 trillion in unrealized gains. Many Investors are wanting ways to defer those gains and finding the right opportunity zones to invest in.

Puerto Rico has been largely overlooked by American and Global investors alike. However, with tax incentives galore and property values so low, the real estate market of Puerto Rico might represent a gold mine for people who are willing to invest on the island. However, as you have seen, there are some essential things to take into consideration if you're thinking of investing in the Puerto Rican real estate market.

Before Hurricane Maria, the island was already in a financial mess and struggling. The real estate market of Puerto Rico had already been following a downward trend for the past several years do to the expiration of its tax incentives to corporations in 2006. After the hurricane, the market further adjusted and created more opportunities for real estate investors. Do to the new tax incentives it is believed that a new emerging market is now in transition. It is a buyer's market and values of homes are at an all time low.

If you are an investor who wants to defer your gains until 2027 and take advantage of the tremendous opportunities at your disposal, then this could be the prime opportunity to invest. Sell high and buy low.

Interest in the real estate market continues to appreciate daily. The local Real estate industry from attorney's to agents are optimistic about the market's ability to recover and thrive.

If you are considering investing in Puerto Rico please feel free to contact us for more guidance and information.

Luis A. del Mazo, Jr.

Tanya Rodriguez

53 Calle Las Palmeras

San Juan, Puerto Rico 00901

615-543-6587

Luis@usrealcoin.us

www.USRealCoin.us

# PUERTO RICO:
## Fools Gold or Gold Mine?

## SHORT BIO:

Luis and Tany have both been active Realtors and Real Estate investors since 1998. Both have worked all facets of the industry. In the last year, they have traveled the world attending conferences from New York to London, studying the economic climate and where investors and capital are flowing. After meeting with Bankers, Lawyers, accountants and Fund managers they have found some similar opinions and viewpoints on where the future of Real Estate investing is headed. Today Luis and Tanya live and are doing business in Puerto Rico and want to bring its up and coming Real Estate market to investors worldwide.

Visit their Website at www.usrealcoin.us
for more information

ISBN 978-0-359-67807-5

90000

9 780359 678075

www.ingramcontent.com/pod-product-compliance
Lightning Source LLC
Chambersburg PA
CBHW020957180526
45163CB00006B/2402